The Third Book of Chester Motets
Revised Edition

The Spanish School for 4 voices

Edited by Anthony G. Petti

LIST OF MOTETS

CHESTER MUSIC

EGO SUM PANIS VIVUS

I am the living bread which came down from heaven: whoever eats
this bread shall live for ever. Alleluia. (*John,* vi, 58.)

Juan Esquivel (late 16th cent.)

CANITE TUBA

Sound the trumpet in Sion, for the day of the Lord is near. See, he is coming to save us: winding paths will be made straight and rough places smooth. Come, Lord, and do not delay. (*Joel,* ii, 1; *Isaiah,* xl, 4.).

Francisco Guerrero (1528–1599)

8

GLORIOSE CONFESSOR

Glorious confessor of the Lord, blessed Father Dominic, living an angelic
life on earth, you have become a paragon of virtues for the world.

Francisco Guerrero (1528 – 1599)

PECCANTEM ME QUOTIDIE

The fear of death frightens me, who sin every day and do not repent. Because there is no redemption in hell, have mercy on me, God, and save me.

Cristobal Morales (c. 1500 – 1553)

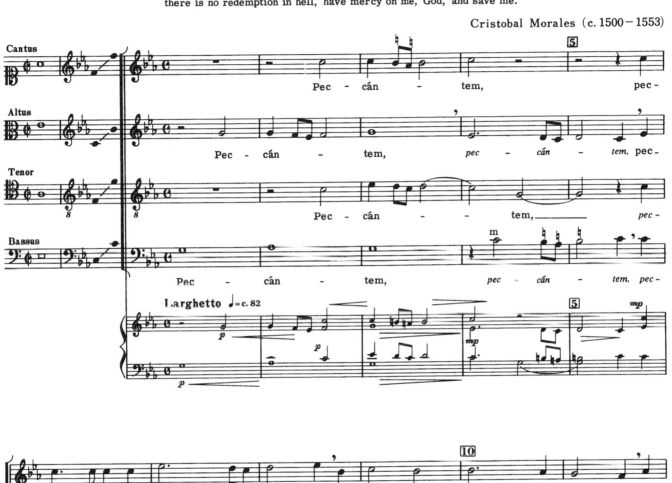

REGINA CAELI

Queen of heaven, rejoice, alleluia: for he whom you were worthy to bear has risen
as he promised, alleluia: pray for us to God, alleluia.

Cristobal Morales (c. 1500 – 1553)

SIMILE EST REGNUM

The kingdom of heaven is like a householder who went out early in the morning
to hire labourers for his vineyard. And he went out about the third hour and
saw others standing idle in the market place and said to them: "Go also into
my vineyard, and I will pay you whatever is just". (*Matthew*, xx, 1, 3, 4.)

Cristobal Morales (c. 1500 – 1553)

JANITOR CAELI

The Keeper of the gate of heaven and the Doctor of the universe, judges over the
ages, true lights of the world: one triumphing by the cross, the other by the sword,
have attained crowns in the court of eternal life.

Diego Ortiz (mid - 16th cent.)

ANIMA MEA

My soul melted when my beloved spoke. I have sought him and not found him, I
called and he did not answer me. I beseech you, daughters of Jerusalem: if you
find my beloved, tell him that I am languishing for love (*Song of Songs*, v, 6, 8.)

Martin de Rivaflecha (d.1528)

28

AVE MARIA

Hail Mary, full of grace, the Lord is with you, blessed are you among women
and blessed is the fruit of your womb, Jesus Christ. Holy Mary, Mother of God,
pray for us sinners now and at the hour of our death. Amen.

Tomas Luis de Victoria (c. 1548–1611)

O MAGNUM MYSTERIUM

How great a mystery and wonderful a sacrament that beasts should see the new-born Lord lying in a manger. O blessed Virgin, whose body was worthy to bear the Lord Jesus Christ. Alleluia.

Tomas Luis de Victoria (c. 1548 – 1611)

O VOS OMNES

All you who pass by, stop and see if you have witnessed any sorrow like mine. All you nations, stay and look upon my sorrow. (*Lamentations*, i, 12.)

Tomas Luis de Victoria (c. 1548 – 1611)

[𝄋 Si est dolor *ut supra*]

PUERI HEBRAEORUM

The Hebrew children spread their garments in his way and cried out saying,
Hosanna to the Son of David: blessed is he who comes in the name of the
Lord. (*Matthew*, xxi, 8, 9)

Tomas Luis de Victoria (c. 1548—1611)

EDITOR'S NOTES

While the madrigal is now coming into its own in terms of individual editions and collections, the motet is still somewhat neglected, and has even suffered a setback, because the disappearance of Latin from the Roman Catholic liturgy has caused many works to go out of print. Musicologists continue to introduce new editions, but their main emphasis is on the provision of larger scale works for the concert hall or of scholarly editions which are often beyond the scope of the average choir to decipher and transpose, let alone sing.

The aim of the present series is to make more readily available a comprehensive body of Latin motets from the Renaissance period, combining old favourites with lesser known or hitherto unpublished works. The first five volumes are arranged nationally, covering Italy, England, Spain, Germany and Slavic areas, and the Low Countries; and each contains, on average, twelve motets drawn from not less than six composers. They are for four mixed voices, and should all be within the scope of the reasonably able choir. They also provide a fair selection from the liturgical year, as a guide for the church choir and for performing choirs who like to present their music according to theme or season.

The editor has endeavoured to preserve a balance between a critical and a performing edition. The motets are transposed into the most practical performing keys, are barred, fully underlayed, provided with breathing marks, and have a reduction as a rehearsal aid. Editorial tempi and dynamics are also supplied, but only in the reduction, leaving choirmasters free to select their own in the light of their interpretation of a given piece, vocal resources and the acoustics. The vocal range for all parts is given at the beginning of each motet.

As an aid to musicologists, the motets, wherever possible, are transcribed from the most authoritative source, and the original clefs, signatures and note values are given at the beginning and wherever they change during the course of a piece. Ligatures are indicated by slurs, editorial accidentals are placed above the stave, and the underlay is shown in italics when it expands a ditto sign, or in square brackets when entirely editorial.

Each volume includes a brief introduction concerning the scope of the edition, with notes on the composers, the motets, the sources, editorial emendations and alterations, if any, and a table of use according to the Tridentine Rite.

16th century Spanish polyphony is obviously very rich in quality and quantity, but there is as yet no comprehensive picture available, despite recently renewed efforts to collect and edit it. Victoria has long been held in high esteem and has been accessible since the time of Felipe Pedrell, but not even Morales and Francisco Guerrero, the other two great names that immediately spring to mind, have received adequate treatment. That there was such a strong tradition in Latin church music in Spain is only to be expected of a country which was the mainstay of the Counter-Reformation not only in the field of power politics but in devotional fervour also. In the reigns of Charles V and Philip II especially, the patronage and encouragement given to church musicians was considerable, and each large local community fostered a strong musical tradition. Every aspect of the Roman liturgy was amply supplied with settings, with innumerable Masses and a wealth of Marian music in the form of Magnificats, motets and antiphons. The disposition of composers given here reflects the editor's sense of hierarchy for the major ones, and his attempt, in the case of the lesser known composers, to provide a reasonable chronological spread and a sense of variety in the type of liturgical texts set.

Juan Esquivel, who flourished around the beginning of the 17th century, is the latest composer represented. He was a pupil of Juan Navarro and succeeded him as chapel master at Ciudad Rodrigo, and was handsomely patronised by the bishop of that diocese, Pedro Ponce de Leon, who subsidised his publications. Esquivel's compositions include a volume of masses, published 1608; motets for four, five, six and eight voices, which also appeared in 1608; a lost publication of psalms, hymns, antiphons and masses (1613); and a number of works in manuscript. *Ego Sum* is to be found in a volume mainly of his motets in Plasencia Cathedral (MS. 1), and it is also included in the 1608 book of motets. Esquivel often makes deferential allusions to the works of distinguished Spanish predecessors and contemporaries, and it is possible that the *Ego Sum* owes a little to the Victoria setting. The piece also seems to be influenced in places by Palestrina in its patterning of fugues and its well-sustained and symmetrical melodic phrases (cf. Palestrina's setting of *Ego Sum*). It is reminiscent, too, of Marenzio in the general movement and sequence of the alleluias, especially in the way the voices are paired. The work has three almost equal sections. The first opens with an apparently copybook style fugue at the fifth and in the Aeolian mode, though quickly changing into Ionian with the introduction of F♯ and B♭. The musical phrases follow the verbal contours well, with lengthened or dotted notes for accented syllables and with gently descending step phrases for "descendi" in a form of restrained word-painting. The section "si quis" uses a second fugue at the fifth with a somewhat similar subject to balance the first, and with rising melismas for "in aeterum". All voices come together in a final *fermata* chord before launching into the third section, which is in brisk triple time for a crowning set of joyful alleluias. The piece maintains its liveliness throughout until its final C major cadence. It has a fine sense of integration and is nicely judged in length of statement and degree of emotive emphasis.

Francisco Guerrero (1528-99), who in his day had a reputation far exceeding even that of Victoria, is being rapidly rediscovered as one of the greatest and most versatile Spanish composers of the Renaissance. He received his childhood training in music from his brother Pedro and some tuition from Morales. After being successively chapelmaster at Jaen and Málaga, Guerrero filled sundry posts at Seville Cathedral and eventually obtained the coveted post of chapelmaster there on the death of the extremely aged Fernandez de Castilleja in 1574. He travelled widely, visiting Rome (at least twice), Venice, Lisbon and the Holy Land. His substantial corpus of compositions includes Masses, motets, psalms, hymns, Magnificats, a Te Deum, and a brilliant collection of spiritual songs or villanescos. The motet *Canite Tuba* was published in *Motteta Francisci Guerreri in Hispalensi Ecclesia Musicorum Praefecti* (Venice, 1570). It is the first part of a double motet, the second being *Rorate Caeli*. The writing bears comparison with Palestrina's five-part setting, which it resembles in various ways and probably predates by a couple of years. Some of the melismatic phrasing is the same, for example, at "Sion" and "salvandos". The trio sections for "et aspera", with their contrasts of upper and lower voices, are remarkably similar, as are the paired passages for "veni Domine". Both composers also repeat with little variation the section from "veni Domine" to the end for both the *Canite* and the *Rorate*. However, Palestrina achieves the effect of a fanfare at the opening by three middle voices singing the triad together, while Guerrero uses a fugue in which each part descends the triad. Again, where Palestrina has homophony for "ecce", Guerrero begins a new fugue, this time with a double subject, so that the homophony of "erunt prava" and "et aspera" is all the more striking. The Guerrero setting is also far less exuberant, as if more conscious of ascetic restraint for the Advent season. Thus the Dorian mode is used rather than the more joyful Mixolydian that Palestrina adopts. The final alleluia, the source of so much brilliant colour in the Palestrina, is absent, and both parts of the double motet fade away at the end, closing on a bare fifth, with all voices singing in a fairly low compass.

The *Gloriose Confessor*, is, like *Canite Tuba*, the first part of a double motet, and was also published in *Motteta*, 1570, though it had first appeared in Guerrero's *Sacrae Cantiones*, 1555. In the 1555 edition the saint honoured is St. Jerome ("Hieronyme", bars 14-17) rather than St. Dominic. The motet also survives in a contemporary manuscript source (Valladolid, Santiago Codex) in which "N." (*nomen*) is used in place of a name, so that any confessor's name could be inserted, a practice recommended for this present edition, though the name "Dominice" has been used according to the 1570 underlay. Understandably, this motet was much admired, and was parodied by Esquivel. The texture is smooth and refined, the phrases are well-shaped and tuneful. Above all, there is a consummate ease which gives the work an appearance of deceptive simplicity from the opening clean-cut fugue, through the mainly homophonic invocation to St. Dominic and the clearly articulated and compact fugal subjects for "vitam angelicam", "gerens in terris" and "speculum bonis", to the firm conclusion where the outer parts move in augmentation in a form of *cantus firmus*, whilst the inner ones interweave as in a tapestry, the tenor moving into place last of all in traditional style — all of which features may have had some influence on Victoria.

The "most excellent" Christobal Morales (c.1500-53) was even more famous in his time than his pupil Guerrero was in his, and he too is only now being given the attention befitting his deserts. Among his early appointments were the posts of chapelmaster at Ávila and then Plasencia. In the early 1530's he left for Rome, becoming a singer in the Papal chapel. He was back in Spain by 1545, when he obtained the coveted post of chapelmaster at Toledo Cathedral, though he stayed only a short time. He left for the small Andalusian town of Marchena, where he was patronised by the Duke of Arcos (1548-51), and his final post was at Málaga. Unlike most of his distinguished contemporaries, Morales concentrated almost entirely on sacred music. His compositions include twenty one Masses, a set of Lamentations, Magnificats, the Office of the Dead, and a large number of motets, many of which remained unpublished in his lifetime. The first of the motets provided here, *Peccantem Me Quotidie*, survives in manuscript in Valladolid (Archivo Musical de la Catedral, MS. Parroquia de Santiago). The liturgical text usually brings out the finest in Renaissance composers (cf. the settings of Palestrina and Gesualdo), and Morales has produced a remarkably intense, sustained and climactic setting, reinforced by the repetition of the final section, "Quia infernorum". The modality varies considerably, with a wide range of cadences provided, including the Phrygian cadence with its sense of irresolution. There is also a constant shift from major to minor. As might be expected, prepared dissonance is frequent, especially for key phrases like "timor mortis", and from the very outset there is a case of unprepared accented dissonance in the minor ninth when the alto G clashes with the bass Ab (bar 2). The near-panic of "conturbat me" and the urgency of the supplication "miserere" are both expressed in two sets of block statements, in the second of which all voices move to the higher parts of their register (bars 21-3; 28-31), a technique similar to that used by Jaquet of Mantua. There is also the word-painting of the descent into hell ("Quia infernorum"), with each part stepping down the scale, and the concomitant sense of hopelessness provided by the Bb minor chord in "nulla est redemptio".

The *Regina Caeli*, to be found in the same manuscript as the *Peccantem Me*, is a bright and lively piece. It is also very inventive, even though, like most settings of this text, it is based on the simple plainsong version of the antiphon. The plainsong is treated quite freely, and is handled as a canon at the fourth between the soprano and alto throughout, while the tenor and bass, having begun fugally with their own subject, soon move along their separate ways, apart from an occasional canon or pairing. As a contrast to the fairly measured tread of the two upper parts, they are often quite florid, especially for the alleluia section, when they break into long melismas.

The third Morales piece, the *Simile Est Regnum* survives in two manuscripts, a complete but often difficult to read copy in Toledo Cathedral (Libros del Polifonia), and the other in Granada Cathedral, which lacks the alto. This piece is in a formal polyphonic style which comes later to be associated with the school of Palestrina and those motets of Victoria which use an extended form of fugue. (There are incidentally echoes of this motet in such works as Victoria's *Gaudent in Caelis*, which contains the identical opening phrase). The opening fugue is given plenty of air, but does not move up or down the voices in strict succession, though it is later more conventional in this respect, as in "conducere" (bars 24ff.). The work has a majestic sweep, and each phrase dovetails beautifully with the next. The pace is necessarily maintained throughout this lengthy text until near the end, when, with the husbandman's call to the remaining labourers, the note values are suddenly doubled. But now the treatment becomes homophonic, and the final statement is both emphatic and brief. Particularly noticeable in this piece is the skilful handling of the melodic curve of each line, with just the occasional unusual leap, (as in the major sixth of the soprano in bar 6), and the piece virtually sings itself, much as the Kyrie does of Palestrina's *Missa Aeterna Christi Munera*, which bears considerable resemblance to it.

The next composer, Diego Ortiz (c. middle 16th century), though born in Toledo, seems to have spent most of his composing life in Naples, then under Spanish rule, and was made master of the Viceroy chapel by the Duke of Alva, holding that position from 1550 to 1570. He is celebrated for his treatise on ornamentation in music for viols, published in Rome 1553. His main contribution to sacred music is his collection, *Didaci Ortiz Toletani . . . Musices Liber Primus Hymnos, Magnificas, Salves, Motecta, Psalmos* (Venice, 1565). *Janitor Caeli* is one of the thirty four hymns in this work, and is the second stanza of *Aurea Luce*, a six-stanza hymn to St. Peter and Paul, which was replaced in the breviary reform of 1632 by *Decora Lux* (cf. second verse). There were two basic plainsong melodies to this hymn, which are very similar to the ones used for *Decora Lux*. The normal format for hymn compositions was for the odd verses to be sung in plainsong and the even ones in polyphony, and although Ortiz has set only verse two, it is likely that he intended all the even verses to be sung in the same way. For choirs who would like to preface the setting with the plainsong first stanza, the version which Ortiz seems to have been using is given below. As with most of the hymns he set, Ortiz makes a close paraphrase of the plainsong, and follows it through fugally. The setting is compact, with a defined pulse and a nice sprinkling of melismas to give the work a binding smoothness, and there is some syncopation, mainly in the tenor, for rhythmic interest. The harmony is restrained and frequently spare, with a number of bare fifths and one or two bare octaves.

Martin de Rivaflecha (or Ribaflecha) is the earliest Spanish composer included here. He was born in the late 15th century, and his first important appointment was as chapelmaster at Palencia Cathedral. The post was uncongenial to him, since he was supposed to clothe and feed the choirboys and give them a general education as well as conducting them, and he could be released from these duties only by taking a cut in salary. In 1524 he left for Calahorra but returned to Palencia with the offer of a sinecure and was soon reinstated as chapelmaster. The post continued to be beset with financial problems and he had to engage in a law-suit to obtain his long overdue salary, the litigation being continued by his family after his death in 1528. Although Rivaflecha was highly thought of in his day, he is scarcely given more than a mention in most books dealing with Spanish polyphony. Yet what little is known of his mostly unpublished work seems to indicate that he was a composer of great distinction with a fine sense of melodic line and a warm response to the emotive connotation of the liturgical text. The *Anima Mea* (MS. Columbina, Biblioteca Colombina, Seville) provides an excellent example of his sensitivity to words in its simple, well-sustained and gentle movement, with controlled cadences only slightly ornamented by the alto line, if at all. The first two sections are almost entirely homophonic. The text is lightened in texture and made more personal by the use of pairs ("Quaesivi . . . vocavi") and is followed by two delicate canons for "Adjuro vos" and "si inveneritis". In the final phrase "quia amore langueo", the pace is slowed down, a D minor chord adds wistfulness to "amore", and the sense of languishing is well conveyed by a touch of syncopation, a passing dissonance and the incompleteness of the final dominant cadence relative to the basically Ionian mode of the piece.

Tomas Luis de Victoria (c. 1548-1611) shares an eminence in sacred polyphony with Byrd, Lassus, and Palestrina, though his known corpus of compositions is by far the smallest of that group, and is also confined exclusively to sacred music. He was born at Ávila and entered the cathedral there as a choirboy around 1558. He also probably attended the Jesuit boys' school of St. Giles, which was patronised by St. Teresa of Ávila. In 1565, he went to Rome and entered the Jesuit German College as a seminarian and singer. Within a few years he obtained several important music posts, and in 1572, at the age of 24, published his first book of motets. By 1573 he was music instructor at the German College and chapelmaster in the Seminario Romano, as well as director of music at Santa Maria di Monserrato. He was also for several years a member of the newly-founded oratory of St. Philip Neri, whom he must have known very well. At the same time he had acquired many notable patrons, and was thereby enabled to publish several volumes, including a set of hymns, Masses, Magnificats, motets, and the Office of Holy Week. By 1587 Victoria had resettled in Spain. He became chaplain to the Dowager Empress Maria at the Royal Convent in Madrid until her death in 1603, and choirmaster to the choir of priests and boys attached to the convent. He was also the convent organist until his death in 1611. The long period following his return to Spain produced comparatively little published music: a book of Masses, 1592, a collection of Masses, Magnificats, motets and psalms, 1600, and the Office of the Dead, 1605.

The range of Victoria's style is quite remarkable: a work can be brief, severely chastened and uncompromisingly ascetic as in some of the tenebrae Responses or it can be extended with a wide range of Early Baroque features of rhythmic, melodic and harmonic intricacies as in his works for double choir and continuo. There is always a strong sense of rich sonority and an unfailing sense of deep spirituality, living up to the motto of the Jesuits who educated him: *ad majorem Dei gloriam*. The four pieces have been chosen here not only because of their intrinsic beauty but because they provide examples of the great range of expression Victoria achives even when working within the framework of a four-part setting in conventional polyphonic style. The first piece, the four-part *Ave Maria*, though extremely popular, seems not to have been published in Victoria's lifetime, neither does there appear to be extant either a holograph or even near-contemporary manuscript source, a case analogous to other famous four-part motets: Palestrina's *Alma Redemptoris* and Felice Anerio's *Christus Factus Est*. Though the Bayerische Staatsbibliothek is said to house a manuscript copy, a search there has proved unavailing, and the earliest extant source appears to be Felipe Pedrell's edition in volume VIII of the complete works of Victoria. The work is a remarkable combination of warmth, tenderness and joy. It is introduced by the plainsong intonation of the antiphon in the soprano, which then loosely paraphrases the chant, while the other parts occasionally reiterate it in canon in the free style of the first half of an otherwise mainly homophonic setting. The different vocal combinations are used very skilfully, most markedly in the section beginning "in mulieribus" where the progression moves from two to three and then four parts as the text moves towards the invocation of the Holy Name. In the next section, "Sancta Maria", an antiphonal style is employed in the homophonic writing, and it is suggested that the apparent echo effect be reinforced by using a quartet as indicated in the reduction (bars 24-6, 30-2). Most striking of all is the rhythmic variety and syncopation of the piece which give it not only a particularly Spanish flavour but counteract what might otherwise be a cloying sweetness of melodic line. The syncopation begins quite early but with all parts moving together against the *tactus* (bars 6-7). It reappears for "Jesus", in the three upper parts, with the dotted notes of the soprano giving a fine sense of ebb and flow in a rhythm to be much favoured by Monteverdi in the *Vespers*. The time changes from duple to triple for a brief spell for the invocation and supplication to Mary, not only as a symbol of perfection contrasting the Mother of God with the earthly fallibility of "peccatoribus," which returns to duple time, but also apparently to give a sense of optimistic buoyancy as if the request were granted at the very moment of asking.

The *O Magnum Mysterium*, although an early work (published in *Motecta*, 1572), is considered one of Victoria's greatest compositions, and is pre-eminent even among the settings of Willaert, Byrd, Palestrina and Gabrieli. The awe and wonderment of the liturgical text are conveyed throughout by the sensitive handling of the haunting Dorian mode with frequent Aeolian cadences, and are established from the outset by the slowly evolving fugue in extended notes and the fifth drop, with the mysterious touch of the implied flattened sixth (bar 5) and the delicate melisma in the soprano on "Sacramentum". The opening phrase ends strongly with a homophonic statement — a common trait in Victoria, and used to close all the sections of this work. For the "ut animalia" phrase, much as in the *Ave Maria*, a pair of lower voices is used, followed by a trio of the upper parts, then all four, and finally the upper three again. In "jacentem in praesepio" a gentle, rocking little fugue appears in carefully balanced ascending and descending passages. The second major part of the motet begins with a lengthened homophonic invocation followed by a mixed style, with "portare Dominum" fittingly lightened by the loss of the bass, and a gradual *rallentando* for the Holy Name. Now follows in the third major part a highly rhythmic and syncopated set of alleluias in triple time which fan out into a set of quite florid runs in duple time; but the whole of the alleluia section is so controlled that its joy and exuberance do not completely overlay the necessary sense of reverential awe.

O Vos Omnes (Officium Hebdomadae Sanctae, 1585), one of two settings by Victoria, is a masterpiece of brevity and simplicity, and has a poignant beauty which searches out the quintessence of the grief and suffering of Christ, especially in its continuing sequence of suspensions, with prevalent dissonances of the major and minor second. In section *a*, one voice leads to others in each of the exclamations (bars 1 and 9). The first phrase gains its effect by the sonorities of the lower registers. The second, for "attendite", has leaps in each voice which give the impression of a cry of pain, and ends in a Phrygian cadence of almost unbearable intensity, with the soprano leap of a fourth, and the flattened sixth of the bass against the alto G. The *b* section, "Si est dolor", has a parallel but quieter sense of climax as the opening minor third is layered with the addition of the fifth and then the octave, and the dissonances of the major and minor second follow each other inexorably. Then the section comes to rest in a quiet, almost homophonic conclusion, with a major cadence. The *versicle* has a slightly quickened movement and forms a tense and nervy descant on the "attendite" of section *a*, with the soprano and alto interweaving, and with emotive leaps in the stretto fugue for "dolorem". No sooner has the section ended in a C major cadence than the C minor of the repeat begins, and the agony starts all over again.

The *Pueri Hebraeorum*, also published in *Officium Hebdomadae Sanctae*, 1585, is a particularly ebullient and happy piece with a mood perfectly appropriate to Christ's triumphal entry into Jerusalem. The music makes the most of the narrative description in the liturgical text. The opening fugue gives the impression of a crowd assembling from diverse parts of the city, and the homophonic section for "vestimenta prosternebant" conveys the spontaneous throwing down of garments to line the processional route. The shouts of "et clamabant" seem to come from different sections of the crowd, which suddenly unites for "Hosanna Filio David". The "benedictus" achieves a remarkable sense of climax reached by the F major chord at the end of "qui venit" (bar 51), and the procession sweeps on in a triumphal march until the final stirring cadence. For all his dramatic effects, Victoria has assimilated many features of the plainsong antiphon in this masterpiece of integration.

A plainsong version of *Aurea luce*, verse 1, to be sung before *Janitor Caeli*, if desired.

Aú-re-a lu — ce et de-có — re ró-se — o, Lux lu-cis, o-mne per-fu-dí-sti saé-cu-lum

De-có-rans cae-los ín-di-to mar-ty-ri-o Hac sa-cra di-e, quae dat re-is vé-ni-am

Table of use according to the Tridentine Rite

Motet	liturgical source	seasonal or festal use
Ego Sum Panis Vivus	*Benedictus* ant., Lauds, Corpus Christi	Corpus Christi, Communion
Canite Tuba	Ant. 1, 3, Vespers, 4th Sunday of Advent	Advent
Gloriose Confessor	Ant., St. Dominic, 4th August	St. Dominic; other confessors by alteration of name (see Notes)
Peccantem Me Quotidie	7th respons., Matins, Office for the Dead	All Souls, Funerals, Lent
Regina Caeli	Ant. of Blessed Virgin, Easter to Pentecost	Easter
Simile Est Regnum	Ant. Office for Septuagesima	Septuagesima, General
Janitor Caeli	Hymn, Office of St. Peter and Paul	St. Peter and Paul
Anima Mea	Ant., Office of Blessed Virgin	Blessed Virgin
Ave Maria	Ant. of the Blessed Virgin	Blessed Virgin, Advent Annunciation
O Magnum Mysterium	4th respons., Matins of Christmas	Christmas to Epiphany
O Vos Omnes	5th respons., 2nd nocturn., Matins, Holy Saturday	Holy Week, Lent
Pueri Hebraeorum	Ant., distribution of palms, Palm Sunday	Palm Sunday